ATLANTIC CITY.

ATLANTIC CITY.

§

Its Early and Modern History.

BY

CARNESWORTHE.
«ALEXANDER BARRINGTON IRVINE.»

Philadelphia
WM. C. HARRIS & CO., PUBLISHERS AND PRINTERS, 125 S. THIRD ST.
1868.

Galloway
SOUTH JERSEY CULTURE & HISTORY CENTER
2013.

This edition published 2013 by South Jersey Culture & History Center

South Jersey Culture & History Center, The Richard Stockton College of New Jersey, 101 Vera King Farris Drive, Galloway, New Jersey, 08205

Title: Atlantic City: Its Early and Modern History
Author: Irvine, Alexander Barrington; pseud. Carnesworthe

Additional material Copyright © 2013
ISBN: 978-0-9888731-0-0

Contents:

———

FOREWORD TO NEW EDITION.

In contemporary America, the mere mention of Atlantic City calls forth a host of specific images. Situated at the heart of the Jersey Shore, there is music, food, and gambling galore—every imaginable way for visitors to entertain themselves to the brink of excess. To say that the picture in the late 1860s was somewhat different is putting it mildly. Instead of towering casinos and flashing billboards there were "hot weather theatricals" and seasonal "bath-houses." The "fashionable gaming table" had yet to be introduced.

As antiquated as such a description suggests, the Atlantic City of 1868 was a modern marvel when compared to the wild waterfront it was less than two decades before. And while *Atlantic City* might not bring us all the way up to the present day particulars, it does chronicle, with quirky charm, the city's progression from no-man's-land to trendy resort by the sea. The account has respectable depth and breadth; however, like many histories, it can be rather subjective, with flexible rules about factuality and with an agenda of its own.

In order to gain a better understanding of that agenda, it is necessary to understand the man responsible for writing the history. The title page bears a single, ambiguous name: *Carnesworthe*. A second *History of Atlantic City*, written by A. L. English and published sixteen years later in 1884, identifies Carnesworthe as a pseudonym for A. Barrington Irvine. If English names Irvine correctly, and he almost certainly does, the once-mysterious *nom de plume* gives way to a brief biographical sketch. Alexander Barrington Irvine lived in Philadelphia at the time of the *History*'s publication and married there in 1870, a detail announced in the *Philadelphia Inquirer.* The son of a Canadian minister, Irvine made his living as the editor of the *Philadelphia and Southern Trade Journal* from 1869-72. But most importantly, both the *Journal* and *History* were published by William C. Harris & Co., strengthening the association between Irvine and the text before you.

The connection to trade is a vital one. Free enterprise was alive and well in 1868, and Irvine takes every chance to drive that point home in what appears to be his only literary effort. The correlation, while significant, is not especially surprising; the editor of a major trade journal would understandably have an optimistic view of achieving the American Dream through commerce—and what an optimistic view it was. In his mind, people only had to open themselves to the possibilities of enterprise and build, build, build. Build railroads, build businesses, build houses, just build. Do that, and the tourists would flock to Atlantic City in droves. Irvine's *Field of Dreams* mentality might have been slightly naive, but it was also spot-on in many respects. The *History*'s discussion of the railroad and the city's (then) current population are impressive and fairly indisputable. Based on facts and backed by records, they show the transition from a once-barren wilderness to a popular summer watering hole, all in under 20 years. They built it, and people did, indeed, come.

Irvine's business-mindedness colors his *Atlantic City* with bold, broad strokes, including the way he strategically lays out the text. He knew that good promotional literature, which this is, must be engaging in order to be effective. The opening tales of Portuguese adventurer Leonarda and the Native American Ocean Girl are filled with the stuff of Old Hollywood, nothing short of fantastical fascinations. However, they are not all fluff and whimsy; they also serve a calculated purpose. Irvine understood that starting with something exciting and exotic before breaking out the serious propaganda would create a more receptive audience and, hopefully, pad the bottom line.

The truly engaging aspect of Irvine's text is the fact that once he *does* break out the promotional material, the intrigue factor does not fade. In fact, the only thing woven through the text as thoroughly as his capitalism is his irreverent wit. Even while extolling the virtues of commercialization, he cannot resist throwing in pause-worthy oddities here and there: the crazy captain and his howling mastiff; the remarried widow and her un-dead first husband; the riotously longwinded lead-in to the Gandy murder; the heroic middle-aged female sunbather. He continually refers to the manuscript that many of the stories supposedly derive from as "moth-eaten," "mutilated," and full of "hen-scratches," a kind of tongue-in-cheek anti-assurance that blends exceptionally well with his gently sardonic style.

These curious anecdotes are included in offhanded and matter-of-fact ways, and the effect of that nonchalance ranges from mild skepticism about the reliability of his sources to outright disbelief. However, because the writing is consistently interesting throughout—downright entertaining in parts—determining where fact ends and fiction begins is no easy task. Even though many of Irvine's stories lack substantiation, there is an underlying sense that they are based in reality; the desire to believe them is strong. When tempered with liberal doses of verifiable statistics, these curious accounts create a text that is enjoyable to read, thought provoking, and informative in spite of itself. In the end readers must decide for themselves how much of Irvine's tale rings true, but remember that some of the most compelling histories are best taken with a grain of salt. Or, perhaps in this case, with a grain of sand.

Stephanie Allen

INTRODUCTORY.

If historic truth should be no less sacred than religion, there can certainly be no reason why the history of the fashionable watering place known as Atlantic City, should be less important to the *beau monde* of Philadelphia, than the annals of Bath in the days when Nash shone in the splendor of his gorgeous ruffles, beneath the smiles of the House of Orange, or than those of England's metropolis in the sunny time when Bryan Brummell paddled the pioneer canoe of phantasy upon the stream of London fashion.

How many claims has Absecon Beach upon the inhabitants of the Middle States, and more especially upon the people of Philadelphia. There, beneath the exhilarating influence of the saline air and surging surf, we take our summer's salty solace, and shuffle off the accumulation of fatigue under which a winter's weary work has made us suffer. There, too, we meet our old accustomed friends, not to buy and sell—not to talk horse, grain, or iron with them—not to waste the day in wordy wrangle with them about stocks, bonds, and the fluctuations of the gold market—but we meet them to read, convulsed with laughs, the funny bill of fare of an enterprising hotel keeper, who loves to make amusement for his friends by providing them with food for their risible, as well as for their corporeal appetites, and also by providing them with the true pleasure ever experienced in the poetry of motion at the gigantic hops, where the dancing toe keeps step alike, to the music of the band and the eternal symphony of old Ocean.

There, too, the student and the clerk, rejoicing in the leisure of the summer holiday, delight to kill the heavily hanging time, as they bask in the sunbeams of the school-girls' eyes and ardently wish that summer was eternal—books all buried—the world turned upside down—in order that the pleasures of Absecon Beach and its fleeting amusements might linger to the last of life.

In short, so nearly, dearly and serenely is this now civilized—once wild and savage retreat, connected with all our thoughts of hot weather pleasures—all our dreams of summer joy, that the history here presented will undoubtedly be read by old and young—by saint and sage—by cleric and disciple—for it is, at once, the record of home life and high life, of low life and middle life—the story of joys, pleasures and pastimes—of happy fights with foaming waves—of long-loved walks and lovely drives—all of which are, and have been the product of that mighty and conquering genius, known to us all by the name of American enterprise.

CHAPTER I.

Early History.

The purpose of this book is to place in the hands of our readers the history of Atlantic City, from the far off days, when the savage held undisputed occupancy of the meadows, where are now enacted the scenes incident to civilized pleasure, down to a time that is within the cognizance of the present visitor to old Absecon—we shall recount the changes from savagism to civilization, from lethargy to activity, from activity to the accomplishment of the grand work which energy and enterprise have wrought out, and we shall endeavor at the same time to point out the causes and accidents that produced these happy results in so short a time.

Of the aboriginal history of Atlantic City, little is known. In the latter part of the seventeenth century, a Portuguese adventurer, named Leonarda, who was supposed to be a lineal descendant of Vasco da Gama, was shipwrecked upon the American coast. His crew perished. He, himself, with a few faithful followers was saved a watery grave, through the friendly exertions of some Delaware Indians. After enduring the most severe hardships, these penniless Portuguese made their way on foot to New York city. There, wandering through the town, among other delicacies of temporary poverty, they succeeded in obtaining the "cold shoulder" from the ancestors of the Knickerbocker aristocracy. In this condition of misery they providentially fell in with a Portuguese skipper, who commanded a barque. The sufferers were taken aboard, kindly cared for on their voyage homeward, and after a passage of ten weeks were again in their native land. Leonarda returned to Portugal to find that his lady-love, a young woman of distinction, had died during his absence. The government requested him to write the narrative of his sufferings and adventures. He did so, but would not hear of the publication of his account. His ambition was gone. He lived only for his loving, dark-eyed beauty, whom he had left behind, and now that he had been spared the waves only to endure fresh misery at home, he ardently wished that he had sunk beneath the billows and joined his Bellsicosa in the immortality of affection. Three years after his arrival in his native land he died of a broken heart at Oporto. In his will he desired that the story of his voyage should never be published. The government respected his request and deposited the record in the archives of the bureau of navigation, where it perished in a conflagration, along with other public documents, twenty years since. About thirty-five years ago an American traveler gained access to this quaintly written document. This antiquary describes it as "a sincere and plaintive, but simple story of adventure, which is probably rendered more sad in tone, than it would otherwise have been, by reason of the private troubles that were weighing upon the heart of Leonarda, when he wrote it." From the correct description of the beach, contained in this peculiar parchment, as well as from the frequent mention therein, of the colony of New Jersey, there can be no doubt that the unfortunate shipwreck, of which Leonarda was one of the few survivors, took place at no other spot than Absecon Beach.

The aforesaid American traveler and antiquary, made copious extracts from this valuable record. On his return to America, he deposited these researches, in the custody of the oldest inhabitant of Atlantic City, which at that time contained but four houses. That ubiquitous old lady (the oldest inhabitant) lost the original manuscript some fifteen years ago, but had previously taken the precaution to make extracts in a note-book, into which she incorporated much useful information, concerning wrecks and murders. The writer has fortunately obtained access to these hitherto unfrequented stores of information, and has been assisted in the business of perpetrating history, by many good citizens of Philadelphia, Absecon, and Atlantic, to all of whom he takes this opportunity of returning his sincere thanks from, as Charles Dickens would say, "his heart of hearts." In spite of the plaintive feature that according to the above quoted traveler, pervades the original narrative of Leonarda, that traveler, provided the old woman's note-book be correct, has left behind him many humorous legends, which throw considerable light upon the customs and habits of life of the aboriginal Delawares, who occupied that portion of the coast upon which now stands Atlantic City.

Since the record of Leonarda is no longer in existence, it is of course impossible to gain any reliable information upon this subject, which if not important, cannot fail to be interesting. We have therefore determined to lay before the public, such a specimen of the Indian legends of Absecon beach, as we have, with difficulty, managed to decipher out of the hieroglyphics of the aged matron, who has lived in Atlantic since the year of our Lord 1818, more than thirty years before Atlantic City had an existence.

CHAPTER II.

———

LEGENDARY.

———

Where be the place that has not its romance and its poetry? There exists no nook, no grove, no rivulet, no fountain, no wood, no cataract, which does not hold up to us, through the dim vista of the past, some bright or foul picture. The rough Hellespont cannot move without murmuring forth the fidelity of Hero and Leander; the willow at the tomb of Ninus still weeps over the cruel fate of Pyramus and Thisbe; the vale of Avoca is still haunted by the spirits of the faithful two, who rather than suffer separation, by the interposition of inexorable parents, died in each other's arms, by jumping from a lofty cliff, a spot still pointed out to travelers, as the "Lover's Leap." Other places have their records of murder and cruelty—we prefer to deal as much as possible with such stories and incidents, as awaken our tenderness and pity, rather than those that fill the mind with things terrible and revolting. The inspired by Mantua's muse may sing of war; and the "blind old man of Scio's Rocky Isle" may chant "Achilles' wrath, to Greece, the direful spring of woes unnumbered." Our legendary specimen must teem with the milk of sentiment and pathos, or with none.

The watering-place which we celebrate in prose though but lately known to civilized people, had in former times its sunshine and its darkness. In the mutilated manuscript of the old lady, above referred to, we are able, by dint of perseverance, and after several almost fruitless attempts to decipher her hen-scratches, to give in our own words, but with due fidelity to the original, an Indian narrative of love and war. The events are known to have occurred among the native Delawares of Absecon beach, that is, provided the "Jersey Shore," upon which Leonarda was wrecked, be really the same spot as is understood by Atlantic City—and of this there is barely room for a doubt.

It appears, that while Leonarda was detained among the indians, by his wreck, a civil commotion broke out among the yellow tribe, on somewhat the same grounds as those upon which the Greek heroes, Agamemnon and Achilles quarreled and separated. At the time where-in the startling events about to be related occurred, there was but one tribe in that locality. Not the least enter-taining of the tribe, was a young Indian girl, who loved the brother of the chief, and was beloved by him in turn. Her mother had died shortly after she had given birth to the future *inamorata* of the chief's brother, and at the time of which we speak, she had no near relative left but her father, who was dragging out a miserable life, by reason of a severe wound in the nape of the neck, which he had received from an arrow, and which had now turned into a cancer.

The chief, who happened to be the elder of two

brothers, was much enamored by the Fair Ocean Maid. This was the name by which she was known in the language of the Delawares. He was not long, however, in finding that his passion was not reciprocated, but, that on the contrary, the fair object of his affections, basked in fancied sunshine when his brother smiled upon her, and would much prefer the frown of him she loved, to the smile of one to whom she was indifferent. In this dilemma, the chief, mortified because the glitter of his lofty position dazzled the eyes of the fair red girl, less than the simple look of him she loved, attempted what is always an impossible task, viz: to turn the bent of true affection, and thus win the fair girl by force. He forbade and prevented all interviews between the lovers, and in the spirit of that celebrated dog, that once upon a time occupied a manger, had her strictly confined and guarded in his own wigwam. No prayers on her part, no protestations on the part of her father could shake his purpose. The brother, whom he had hitherto loved, he now hated, and kept under the strictest surveillance and subordination.

The young brother had a goodly number of youthful companions who favored his cause, and who swore to assist him in winning by force and valor, her to whom tyranny had deprived him. The better to carry out their designs, he and they broke off at night from the general encampment, after a fruitless attempt to rescue the Fair Ocean Maid, and having traveled a distance of about four miles, they constructed some wigwams, where they proposed to reside, and immediately set to work in preparing to make a second assault on the encampment of the chief.

Meanwhile, the Indian girl, as is usual in such cases, pined hourly for her beloved, and no allurements on the part of her would-be husband, could incline her in his favor. Whenever he went to the chase, he left a strong body of men to guard his wigwam, lest his gentle and romantic savage should become the prize of his *fraternal* enemy. Among this guard was a young man named Wau-Koo-Naby, who had loved the captive from his childhood. The disinterestedness and unselfish nature of true affection were never better exemplified than in the conduct of this Indian. Though Wau-Koo-Naby knew that she could never be his, yet he would have risked his life to rescue her from the hands of one with whom he knew she could never be happy. One day during the absence of the chief, while Wau-Koo-Naby was talking apart with the fair child of the ocean, he suggested to her the idea of attempting an escape. At the first thought of such an undertaking, her mind wavered. The risk she would run! What if she should be overtaken? And more dreadful than the rest, what if Wau-Koo-Naby should prove false, or set her free, only to demand his own gratification at her expense, as the price of her liberty! But then thought she, this cannot be. How often had she found him true! How wont was he her path to strew, with white men's scalps in deadly mass, o'er which she might in triumph pass. How oft had they been used to walk, and in lonely places talk of lofty deeds and foamy steeds, owned by *their* brawny great grandsires; whose stories told from sire to son, around the old Indian fires, had by their spirit many a victory won. How oft had he, when others stood retarded, her holy virtue bravely guarded, against foul attack. Thus his faithfulness so well he'd proved, that by his love she hoped to win her loved. A plan was soon agreed upon for effecting her escape. What will not love do to gain its purpose? It will hang on a shred, on a straw, on a hair. It will dazzle the fancy more than our grandam, or our Sunday School teacher could ever have done by their glowing descriptions of Paradise. It will cause the stone to weep with it, the tree to sigh with it, and all nature to rejoice or to grieve with it. And indeed the Ocean Girl allowed the thought of her escape, and of her happy re-union with her young lover, to impress itself so deeply upon her mind, that she thought nothing on earth could be so cruel as to thwart her design.

The night chosen for the escape was peculiarly auspicious. Angry Neptune made the sea swell, and Jove thundered forth the artillery of all the gods. Boreas rose in all his mighty power, as if to bid good cheer to the Ocean Girl. The ancient ocean heaved its troubled breast, and its eternal spirit of unrest, seemed to speak for the GREAT SPIRIT and say "from everlasting to everlasting." The chief had been absent at the chase since mid-day, and had not yet returned. The partner of her designs had persuaded his fellow-guardsmen to go to sleep, assuring them that he would keep an eye to his captive, and awake them on the approach of any person near the wigwam. No sooner had the redskins given over their weary frames to sleep, than the watchful pair crept out of the wigwam, and fled with utmost speed, in face of the wind and storm, in the direction in which they imagined they would find the chief's brother. After they had been gone about two hours, they were obliged to take rest in a grove. The rigors of the night had thrown them into a state of complete exhaustion. No sooner were they seated upon the ground, than they beheld lights at a distance, and horses passing and re-passing between them and the lights. They both concluded that the lights were the fires of her young friends' encampment. Why should they think otherwise? The sight of these lights restored the courage of the exhausted couple. They immediately directed their steps whither the watch-fires allured. As they approached the encampment, they called to their friends for assistance. They were as yet, however, too far from the encampment for their voices to be heard, amid the din and clamor that rent the midnight air in the vicinity of the lights. The fires, too, were much farther than their sight had led them to imagine. When they drew closer to the spot where they conjectured their friends were, the noise of prancing steeds and the loud war-cry, told her and her companion that something terrible was on the tapis. The Ocean Girl cried frantically to her supposed friends, to come to her assistance. The warriors despatched two mounted red men to the spot. Whether these men were friends or foes, the red girl and her companion could not decide, for the dense darkness of the night made it impossible to distinguish, at their then distance from the fires, either the features or the dress of the red men. One of the Indians dismounted, and contrary to all the traditional usuages of the redskins, smote Wau-Koo-Naby to the earth with his tomahawk, and thus fell at her side, the companion of the Ocean Girl. The latter swooned at the sight. The dismounted warrior swung the gentle captive upon his horse, jumped on behind her, and conveyed her to quarters that were by no means agreeable to herself.   *   *   *

The moment the guardsmen, who had been placed to watch the Indian girl, awoke and found her gone, they immediately mounted the fleetest horses they could find and hastened to inform the chief of the infidelity of Wau-Koo-Naby. The chief swore by his tribe that the treacherous Indian should no longer live. He accordingly called the warriors together in council, and ordered them to prepare for the recapture of the Ocean Girl. The commotion incident to Indian war movements ensued, and this was the uproar that startled Wau-Koo-Naby and his companion, upon approaching the watch-fires as above related. The chief succeeded, as we have told, in effecting a portion of his purpose.

CHAPTER III.

THE DENOUEMENT.

The rough sea had brought on a calm, fine morning. The air was cool and refreshing. The birds' merry song could be heard from the wigwam, and the stormy billows that had been all night long, so furiously lashing old Absecon beach, had at last sunk into the bosom of the ocean, and the wide expansive sea was level and bright as a mirror. Already the gorgeous sun was flashing golden blessings upon the beach, and forcing its wakening light through the openings of the wigwam, where the Ocean Girl cast her æiliad piercingly, and beheld sitting at the entrance of her habitation, in sullen, pensive mood, the very man, whom of all others she least desired to see—the chief. Her heart sank within her. Uttering a smothered groan, she hid her face in her blanket. Then back upon her sorrowing soul, came like foul spectres all the deeds and sufferings of the preceding night. Could it all have been but a dream? she asked herself; and wishing for an affirmative reply, she was about to raise her eyes to heaven, to thank the Great Spirit, that she had passed through no dread realities—that Wau-Koo-Naby lived—when those eyes, raised to thank heaven that no life had been taken, caught sight of her companion's blood upon her arms and hands.

She again groaned, and gave vent to sorrow in tears, such as Namaoke shed, when the "poor Indian woman" lost her child. Although the chief at first felt infuriated by the Ocean Girl's attempt at an escape, yet, in the luxury of her eyes, his anger easily cooled, and he vainly spent the day in straining stratagems and making passionate persuasions, in the hope of reconciling his captive to her miserable lot. That night she could not sleep. She had no fear in the chief's presence, for the honor of the red man always prevents his taking advantage of the other sex. Her restlessness was caused by continuous thoughts of him she loved, crowding upon her. Would she ever see him again? Had he been killed in battle since last they met? Did he still think of her? She hoped so, for she could not help thinking of him. These, and a hundred other thoughts occupied her musing, when the noise of advancing horses struck upon her ear, and the air was rent with the wild yells of the aboriginal warriors. Her breast heaved for a moment and then her eyes lit up with hope. It was the chief's brother coming to rescue her. The encampment was speedily roused, and a terrible fight ensued. Her lover's attempt to free her from the chief's bondage was unsuccessful. The chief, however, was slightly wounded in the affray, and would have lost his captive, but for the precaution of an old Indian. The latter disguised her in male attire, and lashed her to a horse, which, during the assault he ever held beside him. During the fight, her lover rode beside her many times, and taking her for a man, made several daring dashes at her with his tomahawk, all of which the crafty old Indian skillfully guarded off. The skirmish, which was commenced after midnight, lasted until daybreak next morning, when the younger brother and his men, overcome by the superior forces of their enemy, were obliged to retire to their wigwams, fatigued and disconcerted. The suffering captive, the object of this fighting and bloodshed, was taken from her steed almost lifeless. Her tender limbs had been cut and strained by the bandages with which the old ruffian had tied her. When placed upon her couch in the chief's wigwam, her frame trembled, a cold sweat coursed through her inmost bones. Her bodily suffering, though severe enough was small, compared with the mental anguish she endured in thinking that her *heart* was murdered. When quiet again reigned in the encampment, the chief approached the Ocean Girl, drew close to her couch and looked inquiringly in her face. That face was placid; not a feature moved, the brow was cold. He caught her hands to rouse her, but they dropped beside her as though they had been lead, and remained cold and motionless. The chief's heart was struck with compunction; all the proverbially noble nature of the red skinned warrior returned, and falling upon his knees, he called aloud to the Great Spirit for forgiveness.

The chief was sorely agitated in his own mind. He had broken the heart of the Indian Girl, and had hated his brother. He could not hope to win the Great Spirit's favor, until he had done *all* that could now be done. After covering with pious care, the body of the Ocean Girl, he rushed from his wigwam and fled to his brother's encampment. He threw himself before Meanemah (for that was the young brother's name), crying "Mercy! Mercy! I have killed the Ocean Girl."

Meanemah raised his tomahawk to dash down the chief of the yellow tribe, when an old Indian stayed the blow, and wrenching the tomahawk from his hand, whispered something in his leader's ear. "No, no!" cried Meanemah, "The red man must not raise his hand against any of the yellow tribe. You are my brother; I spare you not for that, but that you are my brother in the tribe; I this day could send your soul back to the Great Spirit."

The chief himself was overwhelmed, and determined to kill himself. He inflicted a wound upon his breast and fell upon the ground. Meanemah rushed from the wigwam and ran to the chief's habitation, to embrace in death, her, who in her life had been forced from his arms.

What must have been his joy, when, upon arrival at her couch, he found the Ocean Girl, more beautiful than ever, enjoying a gentle slumber. When the chief imagined her dead, she had only fallen into a heavy swoon. The wound which the chief had inflicted upon himself did not prove fatal. He was restored to health and vigor under the efficient care of the medicine men.

So far from regretting his mistake, he rejoiced at

its result, and thanked the Great Spirit that everybody was happy. He resigned the chiefship in his brother's favor, and resolved to live a tranquil life, which we know he succeeded in doing, at least up to the time that Leonarda left the settlement, along with his Portuguese Meanders, to face the hardships of the pedestrian journey, as above related.

The young man, who had assisted the captive in her flight, though he had been severely wounded, yet survived and was requited for his fidelity, by receiving in marriage, the hand of the chief's sister.

This is the first and most interesting story we are able to glean out of the moth-eaten manuscript before us, with the exception, perhaps of the one immediately succeeding it, which, were it not that the thread is broken by the loss of a few leaves in the most important part of the narrative, we would take pleasure in submitting to the perusal of our readers. The other stories are of a predatory character, and would tend more to grate than gratify the reader's ear. This one, however, answers our purpose. It suffices to let us know something of the character of the original inhabitants of Absecon beach.

CHAPTER IV.

Natural Features—Projected Railroad.

When upwards of one hundred years after Leonarda's departure from the New World, the white man first came to settle upon the barren beach, the traces of Indian habitation were few and far between. The place was pregnant with swamps, sand hills and game. This last consisted of foxes, rabbits and wild fowl. An occasional bone poked from a sand-hill, or an old skull found sunk here and there in a swamp, were all the vestiges left to mark the spot, where a century before, deeds of valor had been done, and scenes of aboriginal love had been enacted.

It is impossible to conjecture the cause of the desertion of this place by the Delawares. Whether they dreaded the encroachments of the sea, or the advancing avalanche of pale-face occupation, will ever remain a mystery. Certain it is, that the Indians must have been unknown to Absecon beach, at least fifty years prior to its settlement by Jeremiah Leeds, Adams the agent, and the antiquated saltworks, that long remained a silent monument of defeated enterprise.

The earliest white inhabitant of whom we have any knowledge, was the owner of the above mentioned saltworks, and his family. These people must have existed on the bleak shore for a short time prior to the arrival of old Jeremiah Leeds, who found his way to the spot in the year 1818. From the widow of this pioneer, a lady who now enjoys a green old age, the writer has succeeded in obtaining much valuable information, which has been incorporated into this volume. These early settlers subsisted for a long time on the game, in which the beach even to this day abounds. Squatter sovereignty was the law of the place, and well was such supreme power regarded at that early time, by the primitive whites; although the advantages which that power conferred were not so shrewdly turned to account as they might have been. Up till the year 1852, when the Railroad project was first mooted, the place was regarded as a succession of barren sand hills and unproductive swamps. It was the resort of the ruthless wrecker, whose chief delight lay in alluring, by false beacon, the storm-tossed mariner upon the dangerous Charybdis, in order that the amphibious burglar might reap the reward of his treachery. The news of a wreck was always spread through the interior to the extent of about ten miles, but as we have devoted an entire chapter to "the Wrecks," we shall not enlarge upon the effects which this news invariably produced. With such a class of people living in the neighborhood, it is not surprising, that every mention of improvements was listened to with eager, but jealous ears, by the inhabitants of the six houses that were then upon the island, for from 1818, down till the year 1852, in addition to the saltworks and the house of Leeds, the place had only been amplified by four houses.

During this period of thirty-six years, the beach presented to the unscrutinizing eye of its inhabitants, nothing better than a vast unavailable waste. The keen perception, however, of Dr. Jonathan Pitney, of Absecon, at once detected the peculiar advantages which such a spot offered for bathing purposes. He came, he saw, and his mind conquered the problem. In the extent of the beach, in its gently shelving nature, and smooth and solid sand bed, which produces a gradual declivity, that robs the dreaded ground-swell of its terrors, Dr. P., twenty years before the railway was thought of by any brain but his own, beheld the physical advantages thus presented to the timid aquarian, to frolic in the breakers with impunity. But, although the railway problem was already solved in his mind, the Doctor had to fight many obstacles, among others, that of deep rooted prejudice, before he could succeed in gaining the ears of capitalists.[*]

In some points of the beach, there exists, at a little distance from the water edge, an outer sand bar. This effectually neutralizes the effect of the surf swell, and enables those, whose salubrity suffers by the shock of the surge, to enjoy a bath in smooth water. Upwards of forty thousand Philadelphians annually enjoy the

[*] For an account of the railway, and the difficulties it encountered, see the next Chapter.

pleasant advantages which the glorious summer gives them in Atlantic City. All these pleasures and advantages of which we now enjoy the full fruition, were present to the mind of Dr. Pitney, long ago. When a wild waste stretched before him for ten miles—when upon that waste there were but six residences for man—when the only individuals, that ever lent a temporary increase to the population of the apparently god-forsaken locality, were either the swarming wreckers, ever eager, ever gluttonous, or the wandering sportsmen from Philadelphia, who sought to find the gratification of their desires for game, in a place that man had apparently discarded—when a man's reason was almost doubted, if he were so Quixotic as to suggest that such a place as Absecon beach might be made not only to serve the interests of civilization, but was capable of being both improved into a city of importance, and rendered a formidable rival to the watering places of the country—when the ignorant regarded enterprise in the socialistic light of theft—then was the oracle of enterprise from the mouth of Jonathan Pitney, heard exclaim, "I shall build upon this wild waste a second Cape May."

CHAPTER V.

The Railroad Record.

At the time when Dr. Pitney first conceived the notion of building a railroad over the meadows of Jersey, for the purpose of connecting Philadelphia with the sea, it was opposed to his proposal, that it would be impossible to draw the people away from Cape May, then the favorite resort. The Doctor's long acquaintance, however, with the Jersey shore, had taught him that Absecon beach was a much more accessible spot than Cape Island. He knew that the journey from Philadelphia to Cape Island lay over a rugged and unsatisfactory upland grade. The scenery, too, was at that time rough and uninteresting, presenting a continued and monotonous aspect of the worst kind of farm country, that belongs to a race proverbial for "saving the fractions."

By continued and earnest advocacy of his darling scheme, the Doctor finally succeeded in obtaining the favorable consideration of monied railroaders, who lent their countenance to the proposed enterprise, so far, as to hold a preliminary meeting, and appoint Dr. P. to engineer a bill through the New Jersey Legislature. The faith, however, both of these capitalists, and the people of Absecon, in the ultimate success of the project, was not of a very strong character. The people along the proposed line heard every mention of the coming railroad with derision. Their conduct was a repetition of that of the Fourierites and Socialists. The subsequent history of the road in its organization, subscription to capital stock, and in some other respects, is the old story of the antagonism existing between enterprise and staple stupidity. "Build your road, and the people will starve to death when they get to the beach," said a Jerseyman. "We shall bring over the iron track the food with which to feed them," was the reply of the Doctor. "Build your city, and the winter tides will sweep it away," said the same cent-saving specimen of humanity. But the settlers builded a city upon tiles, established barriers, and laughed away the terrors of old Neptune. "People the beach," said another, "and the mosquitoes will drive the summer residents in herds away." To which the Doctor answered: "The salt breeze from the sea will scatter your mosquito pests, and bring healthy cheeks impervious to their sting." These are some specimens of the Jersey facetiousness that was opposed to the railroad.

Mr. Edwin P. Graham, one of the most respected residents of Haddonfield, New Jersey, informed the writer, that in the early days, when the road was first projected, an old farmer declared he had no particular objection to the railroad, and would give the company all the land they wanted *gratis,* provided he could "hitch his market wagon on behind the train on market days."

The result both of the lukewarm faith which capitalists had in the enterprise, and the derision of the people, was, that Dr. Pitney was baffled in his attempt to get a charter. Nothing daunted, however, he returned to Trenton at the next session of the Legislature, and after constant and determined labor,[*] succeeded both in lobbying through a preliminary bill, and in obtaining the requisite charter. From that time, the railroad was a destined fact, and gradually the attention of capitalists was drawn to the advantages, which, as a summer resort, Atlantic City possessed over Cape May.

The Act of Incorporation appointed John W. Mickel, Andrew K. Hay, John H. Coffin, John Stanger, Jesse Richards, Thomas H. Richards, Edmund Taylor, Joseph Thompson, Robert B. Risley, Enoch Doughty, and Jonathan Pitney, to open books to receive subscriptions to the capital stock of the road. The books were accordingly opened at the "Arch Street House," kept by Thompson Newkirk, on the 24th day of June, 1852. Ten thousand shares were immediately taken up, and the books closed before sunset. At six o'clock, P. M. the thirty-eight stock-holders met, and elected the following board of directors, viz: William Coffin, Joseph Porter, Andrew K. Hay, Thomas H. Richardson (who, on the 25th of August, gave place to Mr. J. C. Dacousta), Enoch Doughty, Jonathan Pitney, Stephen Colwell, Samuel Richards and Wm. W. Fleming. One hour later, the directors met and organized their first meeting with Andrew K. Hay, Esq., in the chair, and Samuel Richards, Secretary, *pro tem*. Messrs. Fleming, Richards and Colwell were appointed the first committee

---

[*] In this labor, Dr. Pitney was materially aided by Joseph E. Potts, Esq.

on by-laws. Messrs. Colwell, Coffin and Richards were appointed to select the most favorable terminus on the Delaware. At this meeting, the report of Mr. Richard B. Osborne, the Civil Engineer, who had made the preliminary survey, was adopted. In this report, the prospective advantages of the road are well portrayed; and the sequel has been the almost correct fulfillment of Mr. Osborne's prophecies. As he predicted, Haddonfield, Long-acoming, Hammonton, Great Egg Harbor and other towns, have grown up into thriving and industrial villages.

The proper principles, that should never be lost sight of in all new works, were rigidly adhered to by the pioneers of this railroad. The line and its furniture were carefully adapted to the country through which the road passed. The line was judiciously selected, so that the greatest benefit might be conferred upon the adjacent country and the public in general. The engineer recommended that the line should be as free from curves as possible; and this wise suggestion has to all intents and purposes been acted upon. No monies have been expended, for which the road has not received a full equivalent, and the entire management since 1852, has been characterized by the absence of all outlay for ornamental and unnecessary work. At the meeting of Directors, held on the 13th of July, Enoch Doughty handed in the names of fourteen new subscribers to the capital stock. They were immediately charged a tax of five per cent. upon their investment. The proper contracts were proceeded with, without delay, and the railroad has ever since been a steady success.

The Company next appointed Dr. Pitney and Mr.

Enoch Doughty, to purchase from the heirs of Jeremiah Leeds, who died about the year 1830, such lands upon Absecon beach, as might be required, both for the railway and the other purposes of the Company. The result of the labors of Dr. Pitney and Mr. Doughty was, that two hundred acres of land came into possession of the Railway Company, for the nominal sum of seventeen dollars an acre.

The Company also purchased the sole right of way, in width, one hundred feet. This way is now represented by Atlantic Avenue. The Dr. labored hard to have the avenues, running parallel with Atlantic of the same width, but the Leeds people objected so decidedly, that the other streets that bear the names of oceans, are not more than eighty feet in width, while the cross avenues that bear the names of states, are not more than sixty. The Railroad Company was for a time buying up land in such large quantities, that there was passed by the Legislature of New Jersey, a prohibitory act, which prevented the Railroad purchasing more than a certain amount of real estate.

The result of this restriction, was the formation of a Land Company, the directors and stockholders of which, were the same persons who held those positions in the Railway. This was perhaps one of the wisest movements that the Company undertook, for it has resulted in incalculable benefits, both to the public and the stock-holders. Although so much had been done to foster this enterprise, although it was plain to the capitalist that an opportunity would by this Railroad be afforded the merchant to make his summer residence at the sea shore, while he could at the same time be transacting his business in Philadelphia; although everything indicated that the rough unexplored region, that lay between Philadelphia and the beach, could be made profitable in the production of light fruits; although the road was formally opened on the first of July, 1854; yet, unfortunately, the crisis of 1857 found the Camden and Atlantic Railroad with its track laid, but with insufficient rolling stock, a large floating debt, and with the economical completion of incidental works, greatly embarrassed by the stringency in the money market, that followed close upon the failure of the Ohio Life and Trust Co. On account both of this, and the laudable policy of the board of directors, to invest the earnings of the road in its thorough equipment, no dividends have been as yet declared upon the capital stock of the Company.

The first President of the Railroad was Mr. John C. Dacousta, and the first Secretary was Mr. J. Engle Negus. During the incumbency of these gentlemen, the first mortgage bonds of the Company were signed to the amount of two hundred and fifty thousand dollars. By this means the rolling stock of the Company was considerably increased, and the affairs of the Company gradually improved to such an extent, that with the exception of the temporary lull of 1857, the Railroad has been one continued financial success.

The report of 1867 is at present before us, and through the courtesy of Mr. Custis, the respected Superintendent of the Road, we are enabled to make a comparison of the earnings of the Road, between the year 1867 and those of 1866 and 1860.

The figures are taken from the books of the Company, and can therefore be relied upon by the general public, as affording a compendious, and at the same time, an exact statement of the existing circumstances of the Railway.

The following table is a correct exhibit for the years named, of receipts and expenditures, including all sums laid out in operations, maintainance and cost of equipments, in the various branches of Railroad machinery.

Comparison of 1867, with 1866 and 1860.

YEARS	MILES RAN BY ENGINES	TOTAL RECEIPTS	TOTAL EXPENDED, INCLUDING COST OF NEW CARS	TOTAL OPERATING AND MAINTAINING	RECEIPTS PER MILE RUN	EXPENSES PER MILE RAN	EXPENSES PER MILE IN OPERATING	EXPENDED OF RECEIPTS	PER-CENTAGE OF RECEIPTS EXPENDED
1867	145,268	325,407 33	206,058 39	181,955 85	2.24	1.42	1.25	63.323	55.916
1866	146,302	303,975 22	200,318 47	181,797 88	2.08	1.37	1.25	65.930	59.810
1860	114,532	160,042 87	105,181 44	105,181 44	1.40	.92	.92	65.720	65.720

This exhibit is a most encouraging one to the stock-holders of the Company. Comparing 1867 with 1866, we find the former year exceeds the latter in increase of receipts, by $21,432.11, and an increase of receipts per mile, ran by trains, of sixteen cents. The cost of running and maintaining the road, has been less than 56 per cent. of the receipts. Such a result is seldom obtained in even those roads doing the largest business. A table recently prepared for the Central Pacific Railway, gives the percentage of receipts expended in operating twelve of the principal railroads of the country. The lowest attained is sixty-one and eight-tenths per cent., by the Reading Railroad. The next in order, is sixty-three and one-half per cent., by the Michigan Central Railroad. The others ran up to eighty and twenty-nine one-hundredths per cent.

Again, the comparison between '67 and '60, the year before the war commenced, and a period of comparative prosperity, finds the figures of 1867—the last mentioned year, showing an increase over 1860, of 103 per cent. in the total receipts, and of 60 per cent. per mile, run by trains, while the increased cost per mile is but 36 per cent.

These results, not only for a young road, but for many an old one, would be justly characterized as extraordinary.

During 1866 and 1867, there were two hundred tons of new iron laid each year, which is included in the above operating expenses of those years, as is every item of expenditure, excepting that for actual increase in stock of cars. For a few years, no new iron was laid, but in the two years just named, the depreciation of all perishable improvements, such as engines, cars, rails, &c., was fully repaired, and the cost of these expenses is all included in the above estimates. In future, iron will be laid with much greater promptness than heretofore.

This is what the railroad, that was originally laughed at, has already grown into, but in addition to its own increase, it has of necessity benefited the public, and by reason of it, has grown up the City of Atlantic, which is to all intents and purposes, the creation of railroad[*]

* The present Directors of the Camden and Atlantic Railroad are Robert Frazer, President, Camden Co. N. J.; Stephen Colwell,

enterprise. Before the railroad existed, the people of Absecon village employed themselves in the primitive occupation of carting oysters sixty miles to Camden, through the sands of Jersey. This *active* kind of work, gave employment to the male portion of the people, whilst dredging and fishing were engaged in by both sexes. In those happy days of blissful ignorance, a few dollars per week was an earnest of six days' hard labor, whilst now, the old grandams of the family can earn twice as much per day, by raising chickens for hotel use in Atlantic City, as was formerly the pittance of the head of the domestic circle, after a week's weary work. Had the railroad not been in existence thus early, there is no doubt that the people of the whole section of the beach county, would, in seasons of scarcity, have been in danger of starvation.

The railroad is so inseparably bound up with the prosperity of Atlantic City, that we may have occasion to refer to it, incidentally, in the future pages of this book. Setting, therefore, the reader's mind at rest, in regard to the stupid farmer, by informing the public that the "market wagon has not yet been hitched on behind the train on market days," we respectfully take our leave of the iron horse for the present, hoping that his snort of enterprise, and puff of power, may long live to lend the

A. J. Antelo and W. D. Bell, Philadelphia; Andrew K. Hay, Winslow, N. J.; S. Richards, Jackson, N. J.; Jonathan Pitney, Enoch Doughty, Absecon, N. J.; Joseph W. Cooper, G. W. Carpenter, Camden, N. J.; H. H. Boody, Jas. N. Potter, S. G. Wheeler, Jr., New York. The other officers of the Company, are, G. W. N. Custis, Esq., General Superintendent; Horace Whiteman, Esq., Secretary and Treasurer; D. H. Mundy, Esq., General Ticket Agent, Camden.

music and enchantment of advancing civilization, to the wilds of New Jersey.

CHAPTER VI.

―――――

THE PRESENT CITY.

―――――

The present city is situated upon Absecon Island, a distance of seven miles from the mainland. It faces the ocean to the south-eastward. Atlantic is sixty-two miles by railroad from Philadelphia, and is of easy access, there being two trains daily, to and from the former city, with which there is also direct telegraph communication.

The entire beach was composed of a succession of sand heaps, thrown up by the heavy winter tides; it therefore became necessary to level them, and gravel the projected streets. Continued efforts soon produced graded thoroughfares, possessing a hard and gravelly road-bed. Capital became rapidly invested in the erection of buildings, and Atlantic City now presents to the visitor, all the attributes of a thriving well-appointed "city by the sea."

Approaching Atlantic City by railroad, we enter upon the salt meadows, immediately upon leaving Absecon village. Here the sea-siders are first apprised of their near approach to the ocean, by their involuntary inhalation of the salt air. The effect of such an atmosphere upon the system, is both exhilarating and stimulating, besides being gratefully refreshing, not only to the invalid, but to the robust in health. Passing rapidly over the meadows, a distance of seven miles, we find ourselves in Atlantic Avenue, the principal street of the city, and upon either side of which are erected the principal hotels, boarding houses, private cottages, stores, churches and market houses. The passenger cars of the railway pass slowly up this broad roadway, on which they stop opposite each hotel sufficient time to allow passengers to alight. By a judicious system of regulating the stoppages, each hotel is placed upon the same footing as its neighbors, so that passengers are alternately delivered at the lower and upper end of the city.

From any position of the island, the view of the sea is unobstructed, and as Atlantic City faces the south, from which come the prevailing summer winds, there is invariably a direct sea breeze during midsummer, and the air is so remarkably dry and pleasant, that invalids who are unable to remain at other watering places on account of the dampness of the atmosphere, derive great benefits from the clear pure air, for which Atlantic City has become proverbial.

The growth of the sea-girt city has been extraordinary. The population during June, July and August, is about thirty-five to forty thousand people. There are three churches—a Methodist, a Roman Catholic and a Presbyterian, two Aldermen, a City Clerk, a Mayor, and all other concomitants of civic importance.

Thus, enterprise, the best of conservatives, because

the best leveller of old abuses, and the best conservator of existing benefits, has levelled the sand hills, dried the swamps, laid out the town, and upon the land has built a city, the summer population of which does not fall far short of forty thousand souls—and all this has been done in the short space of sixteen years.

CHAPTER VII.

THE LIGHTHOUSE AND THE WRECKS.

The amphibious banditti, that formerly fattened upon the misfortunes of their fellow beings, who suffered the hardships of the wrecks, were familiarly recognized by more civilized people as "Barnegat pirates." These consisted of desperate characters, who in a great measure resembled that small class of "dog-gun-and-nigger poor whites," of the South, who subsisted before the war by shooting and fishing. When wrecks were scarce, and false beacons failed in the performance of their required duty, these diabolical specimens of the *genus homo*, lived the lives of wandering "bummers," peripateticating between Absecon village and the beach, and occasionally oystering and fishing, to preserve the connecting link between the soul and body. They were a set of wretches who cared for nothing animate or inanimate, save their own individual selves. Whenever the news of a wreck reached these people, they, eager for the "main chance," rushed in crowds to the beach. To this day, the visitor at Atlantic will hear of strange, wild incidents, that occurred in years gone by upon this sandy waste. The old stagers, now hanging upon the verge of life, and ready at any moment for their final leap into the unknown yonder, will relate around the evening fires, how the wild, half savage wrecker held sway of all around him, save the waves from which he drew his livelihood—how, crushed and sinking beneath the surf, the wild cry of the death struggle from the doomed wreck, was heard to mingle with the hoarse roar of oaths; how the demoniac yell of fiendish delight emanated from the lungs of the despicable wreckers, while seizing and discussing their ill-gotten spoils. Many of the accounts of wrecks, that have been preserved in the manuscript from which we gleaned the story of Leonarda and the Ocean Girl, are full of both romantic incident and absorbing interest, and although they must lose much of their pith and point, owing to the horribly inacurate and illegible manner in which the manuscript record has been kept, yet we have determined to buckle to the work of solving the Atlantine inscriptions, and of our success the reader alone can be the judge.

The wrecks of which Absecon beach has been the *point d'appui*, are very numerous, and the heartrending circumstances attending them are very many. Though tragedy, sadness and laceration are the principal themes upon which we must necessarily touch when intent upon such a business, yet we are assured that the story of suffering cannot be without interest, but that on the contrary, it can only tend to soften the feelings and render the emotions subservient to the purposes of the Creator.

Since the completion and improvement of the light-house, there have been but few wrecks; and little loss of life has taken place thereby. In 1830, the *"Gherge's Khan"* was totally destroyed off the beach; the majority of the passengers were saved, among whom was a little child of nine years of age, that was afterwards restored to joyous parents who lived far out in the wilds of the then almost unexplored west. Captain Busk, however, who commanded the vessel, committed a determined suicide. When the wreck-boats had been placed safely within his grasp, he spurned the offerings of Providence, and with fixed teeth and a face indicative of strong mental agony, he plunged into the water and sank to rise no more alive. It has ever since been supposed that he lacked the moral courage to face the underwriters. A few years after this, the *John Willets* was a total wreck upon the coast. One man floated ashore who had been frozen to death; and Mr. Robinson, who has since taught school in Absecon village, was another survivor of the ill-fated barque.

In 1845, Captain Faircloyke's *Rainbow* was wrecked, but no person at Atlantic City could give us any details of the attending circumstance, which we know were unpleasant enough.

The next year a most harrowing affair was occasioned in a very simple manner. A small schooner had been wrecked, and when the attention of the beach people had been called to the perilous condition of those aboard, the wreck-boat was duly despatched to render what assistance soever was possible. The tide had gone out, so that there was no risk in attempting to land. As the wreck-boat approached the scene of the disaster, the cries for help were more and more distressing. The confusion became multiplied to such an extent, that although the captain and his few sailors and passengers were soon safely transferred, yet in the midst of the excitement, the skipper's wife had fallen beneath the waves. As the fog was exceedingly dense, the accident was not observed, until the ghastly and bleeding body rose to the surface. Her throat was cut by her own watch chain—an anomalous appendage upon the wife of a schooner captain, but then she came from a land where the softer sex, no matter how poor they may be, always manage to *take* the jeweler in the round of "shopping." The skipper was ever after a disappointed man. Before, he had been lively and jolly, but since the loss of his New England consort, "he could laugh nevermore." He refused to again take command of a ship. He gathered all his earnings together and emigrated to the west. His friends say he is crazy, and indeed they are not without grounds for their supposition; for, in a quiet village, of a quiet county, in one of the great States of the mighty west, and in front of a hotel, you will see a man apparently about fifty-six years of age seated beside a mastiff. The dog always shows more intelligence than his master, who rarely speaks to any person. Though the ex-captain cannot be called a very old man, he is very garrulous, but has "fits of lucidity" at times. It was in one of these fits that we were so lucky as to encounter him. We immediately compared his narrative with that of the old woman, and the two were so substantially the same, that we preferred to relate that of the garrulous "fiftysixer"; and in his own words, so that if it be uninteresting, the reader will please spend his vindictive force upon the "old bore" and not upon the writer. In that seat, in front of the occidental hotel aforesaid, Captain Slowe (for that is his name), passes away each day, except at such times as once in three months he goes on foot a distance of one mile, to collect a little interest upon the money he has lent on mortgage. His usual occupation while thus seated, is reading over and over about a dozen different times, the *New York Ledger*, the *Home Weekly*, of Philadelphia, and the *Lacrosse Democrat*. The old "buffer" peruses advertisements, prospectus, and in fact the entire papers. During his reading, if closely observed, he will be seen at times to look abstractedly from his newspaper, stare at the clouds and exclaim in frantic transport: "Maria! Maria! Watch chain, Atlantic City, *New York Ledger*, help! Mrs. Southworth, help!" If you *watch* him during these performances, it will be found that his wandering ruminations are perpetrated about every three-quarters of an hour; and that once a year, on a certain day at the hour of noon, the mastiff joins in and helps the master, by a terrific howl. Reader! strange as it may appear, that howl is always given on the anniversary of the cutting of the throat of the skipper's wife, and not only upon the anniversary, but at the very same hour in which the last sight of his dead spouse was allowed the poor harmless lunatic captain. This truly is stranger than fiction.[*]

It is not forgetfulness that has kept us thus far from

---

[*] Since writing the above, we regret to learn that the master and mastiff both died upon the same day, one year ago.

introducing the reader to the scene of a wreck, the slightest detail of which cannot but call up our tenderest pity. It was on a cold bleak morning in the severe spring of 1854, that the inhabitants of Atlantic City might behold a stout but disabled barque struggling with the waves, the quicksands and the furious winds off Long Beach, like some brave but weary traveler, who, despite decision and vigor, falls prostrate to the influence of hardship and foul weather. 'Twas but a phase of life. There is no place or person—nothing in life, where we do not discover the quicksands of human misery. We look with pity to-day on the fate that may be ours to-morrow. The *Powhattan*, the barque that now struggles before us, but yesterday buffeted the breakers and rode triumphant, regardless of the trident, now kneels imploringly to the power, which but some hours ago she scorned.

She belongs to Baltimore, and is bound from Havre with a cargo of merchandise, and three hundred and eleven souls, the fated bulk of whom are emigrants. They have left their all behind them, save the small solid solace needful to start new life in the New World. They have left the old and the very young at home. Some, too, have left their little ones behind them in the ancient world, and some brave hearted fellows have left their wives, in the determination to carve golden happiness from the mines of the widely puffed California. They start out with high hopes of bright and happy days. In their fond fancies, the golden gates of futurity open, under the pressure of gilded rocks, resplendent for their reception. The fair weather and unmackereled skies, feed their embryotic appetites with the pleasures that are to be in the "good time coming." For several days they enjoy reveries of such delectable opiatism. But, in the midst of enjoyment we are in sorrow, and the bright sunshine of to-day's pleasure is changed to the murky misery of the morrow. When the *Powhattan* is eighteen days upon old Neptune's main, the captain's usual suavity of manner has forsaken him, he wears a firm, determined aspect, the signs of an approaching storm are visible in the heavens, ere long the elements are aroused, and a terrible gale is blowing from the northeast. The barque is driven ashore off Long Beach. The wreckers are for a moment in high glee, in the hope that the sorrows of the *Powhattan* may be their own enjoyment. A snow shower comes on, the ship is tossed from stem to stern, the cries of the passengers are heard upon the shore, but it is death to man the wreck-boat. A few resolute spirits, whose judgment is put in abeyance to their feelings, assume the arduous task, and make their way toward the doomed vessel. The rest of the narrative we give in the words of the captain of the wreck-boat:

"When we arrived within about 200 yards of her, the wind had veered, and the sea ran so high that we were unable to pull the boat any further, notwithstanding all our exertions. This was about six o'clock in the evening, and the vessel had first been visible on shore at about noon on the same day. Finding further progress impossible, and fearing for the boat's life, we let go one anchor and showed a light, which was joyfully answered; this we repeated three times. We afterwards beheld the crew assembled on the quarter-deck, when they uttered a dreadful shout for assistance and fired two muskets. Soon afterwards they were seen apparently in great consternation, hurrying about the decks. Presently they were seen to set fire to a tar cask. This made an excellent signal, and had the movement been made at first, we should have been able to render them assistance. As it was, we made the best signal we could for them to lower their boat and make for us, but as they did not attempt it, we have reason to believe that their boats had been carried away. The light kept burning till about eleven o'clock, when the sea broke so heavily over them that it disappeared. Next came on a terrific snow shower. The white flakes thickened every instant; more and more the wind whistled, as if in piteous mockery of the sufferers; the sea rolled furiously and lashed the fated ship." The cries from the *Powhattan* at this time were terrible, and all the attending horrors—the darkness of the night, only relieved by the falling snow, the curses of the wreckers on shore, and the fearful shouts of distress from the barque, would have afforded another "blind old poet" an excellent theme for immortalizing Atlantic City in a new production upon the horrors of the *poluphloisboio thalasses*.

The captain's narrative proceeds: "At about twelve, midnight, the barque capsized, and we had the distressing spectacle of the unfortunate emigrants and crew perishing, without being able to render them any assistance. Their last cries were beyond description. In a few moments she broke up, and we were surrounded with wreck, but could not find any of the crew. From a chest picked up, she appears to have been the *Powhattan*, of Baltimore, bound from Havre, with a cargo of merchandise, and conveying three hundred and eleven passengers."

To give a detailed account of all the wrecks that have occurred upon Absecon and Brigantine beaches, would be impossible within our present space, neither would it comport with the object of the book. A list of the most important ones must suffice the reader.

The *Santiago di Cuba* ran ashore on Long Beach, in the fall of 1867. Seven persons were drowned, including three women, two sailors, a girl, ten years of age, and her mother. The child's body was washed ashore some days after the catastrophe. The corpse was kept until such time as a zinc coffin could be procured, and communication made with deceased's relatives, who at that time lived in Delphi, Illinois. When the grandfather of the child, an old man about seventy-five years of age, heard of the fate of his daughter and grand-daughter, he became hopelessly insane, and died six weeks after the sad news reached him. A Welshman rescued from the ship, returned to his own country, and an Irish girl that had accumulated a small fortune in California, was among the misfortunate seven on the present occasion. The other female, who was consigned to a watery grave, was a southern lady, that had been married but a few weeks. The people of the beach report that her husband became unmanned. He mourned and moaned for his wife, and like Rachel sorrowing for her little ones, "refused to be comforted" because "his wife was not." About three months afterwards, a Michigan woman, whose husband had been missing for some time, appeared at Atlantic City, and with the most perfect *nonchalance*, made inquiry concerning the sailors that had been lost. The body of one had been washed ashore, and a description was given her, so far as such a thing was practicable. She concluded that the description answered completely to her "long lost" husband, and proceeded to calculate how much he should have drawn in the way of pay since he left her, provided he had joined the ship about the time their connubial bliss proceeded upon a journey in an elevated direction through a spout. She also conjectured upon the propriety of remarrying. She did so. She succeeded in obtaining from the vessel's owners the back pay due her liege lord—retired to Michigan, and took to herself a husband. These proceedings showed her strong-mindedness, on account of the "despatch" with which they were taken, and clearly demonstrated the right of women to the ballot. But the nicest schemes of mice and men are often doomed to a cruel counteraction, and how consciously if not conscientiously must she have stood confounded, when, in about six weeks, her dead determinor disgusted her with his *debut* from the section or sphere of the spirits. She did not sing "Home, sweet Home," but she cursed that individual soundly for the hallucination he had practised, to restore her rejected relative. She has changed her religion from Spiritualism to Swedebosity (a modified form of the same complaint), and though she clings to husband No. 2, she declares that were it not for an embryotic connecting link, she would *cut* both husbands, and retire to the spirit world, where she might find her congenial *alter ego*.

Another wreck, that of the *Polly Whimple*, took place

sometime prior to the last mentioned. A stupid attempt was made to land before the tide went out. The result of this fool-hardy enterprise, was, that a boatful of women was swamped, and that several men lost their lives in fruitless attempts to rescue the women. A rich lady who had about one thousand dollars' worth of rings upon her fingers, would have been drowned, but for the heroic conduct of a waterman, who risked his own life to save hers. The same brave fellow was drowned in an attempt to save another woman's life. The husband of the wealthily ringed woman had not even thanked the sailor for bringing him his wife, and now that he was drowned, the Dives aforesaid, never so much as enquired where the sailor's family resided, or whether they had been left in destitute circumstances.

The schooner *General Scott*, was wrecked off Long Beach in 1840. The captain was the only person saved, and he floated ashore upon a feather bed, upon which he must have had a roundabout journey of more than fifteen miles.

On January 13th, 1856, the *Charles Colgate*, of New York, ran ashore, and became a total wreck. The crew, however, were saved by the life-boat.

On the 25th of February, 1858, the *Flying Dutchman* went to pieces at nearly the same spot, where the *Colgate* broke. No lives were lost.

On the 21st of November, 1851, the barque *Baldin*, of Southport, bound for New York, with a cargo of cotton and merchandise, ran ashore, with her mast cut away; and water-logged.

The following list of arrivals at the Jersey beaches, from 1847 to 1856, are as correct a statement as can be made up from the only document before us; and it is almost impossible to be read. Some of these vessels were total wrecks, others got safely off, but as it is not stated in every case, we give the reader all the information we have been able to glean ourselves.

September 29th, 1847, the brig *Patapsco*, laden with molasses, ran ashore on Long Beach.

September 30th, *Ann*, of *New Orleans*, laden with coal, ran ashore on Brigantine Beach.

On the 16th of December, 1847, the schooner *Nile*, ran ashore on Brigantine Beach. She was laden with mahogany. Mss. deficient, consequently it is impossible to relate the results.

On the same day, schooner *Mississippi*, of Hanrich, took shelter in the inlet. She was laden with corn, peas and beans. Mss. deficient. Here there is a long gap in the old lady's account, and the next entry we find, is that of the British schooner *Ida*, Captain Roberts, bound whether for St. John's, N. F., or St. John's, N. B., is impossible to determine. This entry is dated January 2d, 1849. Mss. deficient. On the 25th January, 1849, ran ashore, the barque *Mary Ellen*, of New York. Mss. deficient. On St. Patrick's day, 1849, the barque *Chester*, of New Orleans, Captain Robinson, ran ashore. Mss. deficient. November 25th, 1849, ran ashore, the schooner *Walter A. Merchant*, of Washington, N. C. Laden with naval stores and shingles. Mss. deficient. December 25th, schooner *Brook Haven*, of Newport, from Norfolk, Va., bound to Fall River, Mass., ran ashore. Mss. deficient.

IN 1850.

January 4th, ran ashore, the schooner *Independence*, of Washington, N. C. Laden with naval stores. Got off the next morning. May 5th, schooner *James A. Sanders*, of Hampton, Va., Captain Fennis. Laden with oysters, bound for Staten Island. Mss. deficient. May 6th, brig *Four Brothers*, of Philadelphia, ran ashore, with deck stove in. Load lessened and she got off. May 18th, schooner *Vermillion*, of N. Y. Laden with coal. Got off next night.

Here are the names of several vessels, that cannot be read with any degree of certainty, on account of the almost illegible manner in which the record has been kept.

December 9th, brig *Repplier*, of Boston. Coal; bound for New York. Mss. deficient.

IN 1851.

On January 25th, a New York barque, name undecipherable, ran ashore. Mss. deficient. February (no day of the month given), sloop *Elizabeth Ann*, of Rockaway. Mss. deficient. February 22d, barque *Kirkwood*, Baltimore; Captain Martin. Ashore on Brigantine; from Rio. Laden with coffee. Mss. deficient. April 6th, Swedish barque *Emily*, ashore about six miles below Absecon bar. Bound for New York. Mss. Deficient. August 18th, schooner *Sioux* (Mss. Sio), of Great Egg Harbor. Laden with coal. Mss. deficient. September 11th, *Romaline*, on south side of Absecon inlet. Mss. deficient. October 4th, sloop

Patriarch, of Long Island. Mss. deficient. October 27th, brig *Edward Prexel*, of Boston, ashore. Mss. deficient.

November 21st, brig *Baldin*, of Southport (*vide sup.*). November 16th, barque *Brasalero*, from Cadiz (*Shagirs* in Mss.). Got off next morning.

IN 1852.

January 29th, brig *Wm. Rogers*, of Boston, from Brazil, bound for Boston. Ashore on Absecon bar, north side. Got off same day through the exertions of Ryan Adams. November 16th, schooner *Marshall*, Mss. deficient. November 25th, barque *Mataforda*, of New York, in the inlet. Mss. deficient. December 8th, schooner *Rainbow*. Total wreck. All lives saved but seven (*vide sup.*). December 23d, schooner *Ellen Matilda*, of Calais. Bound to Philadelphia; ran ashore about four o'clock in the morning; got off same night through the exertions of Ryan Adams.

The manuscript has entries of twelve vessels during 1853, but it is impossible to make out whether any of them were wrecked or got off to sea. Also entries of seven vessels in 1854, among which is that of the *Powhattan* (*vide sup.*). Sometime after July, 1855, the *Seaman's Friend* capsized off the beach, and all on board perished before assistance could be rendered them from the shore. The manuscript has nine entries in 1855. The only entry in 1856, is that of the New York schooner *Charles Colgate*, which was a complete wreck, but the crew were saved by the life-boat. We regret, that owing to the irregular manner in which the records have been kept at the beach, we are not able to present a more complete list of the marine disasters that have taken place at Atlantic City. The first note-book that contained the information has been lost, and the manuscript before us is so utterly deficient in details, that we have preferred rather to present certainties, than attempt the elucidation of only possible transpirations.

The great number of wrecks that were continually occurring upon the beach, caused Dr. Pitney to turn his attention to the absolute necessity that existed for the erection of a proper lighthouse at Atlantic City. Again he had to fight prejudice, and especially the prejudice against improvements, that at that time reigned supreme among the grannies of the Navy Department.

Away back between the years 1834 and 1840, the proposal was first agitated. After a great waste of trouble and money, a Congressional appropriation of $5000 was at last voted, upon the proviso, that a satisfactory report should first be made by a competent official of the Navy Department. Commodore La Valette was commissioned to make the aforesaid report. He visited the beach, examined the coast, and requested a letter from Dr. Pitney on the subject. In this letter, Dr. P. explained his own original notion of prismatic lights, for which the French optician, Fresnel, obtained a patent ten years afterwards. Notwithstanding the exertions of Dr. Pitney, the Commodore made an unfavorable report, and the lighthouse project slept for several years.

The Doctor, however, was far from being disheartened by his first failure, and the same pluck that characterized his railroad and land schemes, was again called into play. In 1853, after the railroad had been surveyed, and his hands were in a manner full, he started the lighthouse question again. With his own hands he circulated petitions for signature, and besides wrote to congressmen and published articles in the newspapers, advocating the project. The result of these labors was the granting of an appropriation of $35,000 for a lighthouse, and an additional one of $5,000 for a buoy. Thus, Atlantic has to-day one of the best lighthouses in the country—which, with the recent improvements, cost upwards of fifty thousand dollars in the aggregate. The buoy, however, has disappeared. The contract for this portion of the work was let out to an unprincipled person, who purchased an old flat-bottomed boat, for the purpose of fulfilling his obligations. One stormy night, Proteus took a fancy to this combination of antiquated "wooden walls," and carried it off to the bottom of the sea, where it now quietly remains.

The inlet at Atlantic City has always been a favorite shelter for vessels drawing less than twelve feet of water. The "oldest inhabitant" remembers that one day in the year 1835, one hundred and thirty-six crafts of this description, and again upon St. Patrick's day, 1840, sixty vessels availed themselves of this privilege. The sand bar is at present the only obstacle that lies in the way of Atlantic City becoming a port of entry; but Mr. G. W. N. Custis, the respected Superintendent of the Camden and Atlantic Railway, informed the writer, that the erection of a suitable break-water would in a great measure obviate this difficulty.

The surf has for some years been gradually eating away the land in front of the lighthouse, and without the speedy erection of the necessary break-water, or a deposit of stones sufficient to counteract the influences of the sea, the lighthouse will in a short time stand in imminent danger of destruction. The people of Atlantic, foreseeing this, have united in application to Congress, respectfully soliciting the necessary aid for the carrying out of such works as shall effectually protect the most exposed portion of the island. The beach in one part is so far gone, that the grounds surrounding the lighthouse, are wholly submerged whenever the wind blows with any violence from the east or northeast, and during its continuance, the family of the lighthouse keeper are completely imprisoned, and he and his assistants are compelled to wade through water while discharging their duties. Private property also suffers severely when these inundations take place. It is to remedy these evils that Congress has been petitioned.

CHAPTER VIII.

THE CITY ITSELF—ITS TOPOGRAPHY, &C.

The resident population of Atlantic City is about five hundred. These people, like the inhabitants of Baden-Baden and all watering places, generally *lay off* in the winter, and reap the harvest in the summer. The principal difference between the summers at Atlantic City and those at Baden-Baden, is, that at the former place, the time-killers and pleasure-seekers have not as yet succeeded in introducing that concomitant of European watering place civilization, known as the fashionable gaming table. In other respects, Atlantic City is, if possible, the more entertaining of the two.

It contains a *Mayor*. The present incumbent of this office is the urbane and gentlemanly MR. DAVID W. BELISLE.

The other civic worthies are:

Aldermen: WILLIAM S. CARTER.
                   City Recorder:
                   JACOB MIDDLETON.

SILAS R. MORSE.		JOSEPH A. BARSTOW.
ROBERT T. EVARD.	Councilmen:	JOSEPH H. BARTON.
CHALK. S. LEEDS.		JOSEPH SHINNER.

City Treasurer:	JONAS HIGBEE.
City Clerk:	EDWARD S. REED.

To the last named gentleman our thanks are particularly due for much valuable local information.

The City that, but fourteen years ago, had only one house of public entertainment, now boasts its hundred hotels and boarding houses, its carriages at city rates, its private villas, its thriving railroad, and its by no means insignificant commerce.

The principal hotels are:

SURF HOUSE.	CONGRESS HALL.
UNITED STATES HOTEL.	MANSION HOUSE.

Comfort, tranquility and seaside elegance, can be found in abundance at the SURF. The combination of pleasure, comfort, and the luxury of a shady park, awaits the guest of the "UNITED STATES"; while at CONGRESS HALL, gaiety, hops, jolly life and all the sweets of good digestion wait upon the visitor. Those, who at Atlantic City seek the real pleasure to be derived from nightly hops, card parties, and social amusements, usually patronize the whole-souled, whole-hearted Mr. HENCKLE who, during the past season, has improved CONGRESS HALL, at an expense of several thousand dollars. The SURF, too, holds out all the inducements of a first-class hotel, as well as the happiness of a home.

The other hotels of importance are:

NEPTUNE HOUSE.	CLARENDON HOUSE.
LIGHT HOUSE COTTAGE.	ASHLAND HOUSE.
ALHAMBRA.	GLENN'S INLET HOUSE.
WHITE HOUSE.	KENTUCKY HOUSE.
SEA SIDE HOUSE.	CHESTER CO. HOUSE.
THE YELLOW COTTAGE.	

Persons who desire comfort with small expense, can be well entertained at any of the following establishments:

BEDLOE'S HOTEL.	WEST PHILADA. HOUSE.
PENNA. COTTAGE.	BRADLEY HOUSE.
COTTAGE RETREAT.	SHERMAN HOUSE.
MACY HOUSE.	EXCURSION HOUSE.
REED HOUSE.	GROVE COTTAGE.
ARCH ST. HOUSE.	COLUMBIA HOUSE.
CONSTITUTION HOUSE.	SAND HOUSE.
ATLANTIC HOUSE.	

Besides these we have designated by name, there are about twenty-five smaller houses of public entertainment, including saloons, also about thirty or forty cottage boarding houses. The City possesses a commodious school house, which is a more than ordinary country structure, and contains five departments of instruction. There are upwards of two hundred children upon the roll, and the average attendance is about one hundred and ten. The City raises three thousand dollars per annum for educational purposes. Mr. E. S. REED, the City Clerk, and the druggist of the place, has been the superintendent of the school for the past seven years. The churches, as we have previously stated, are three in number. The Presbyterian and Catholic are of a *Missionary* character, service only being conducted during the summer months. The Methodist, however, manages to keep open "all the year round."

The broad avenues that are called for oceans, run about half-way between northeast and east, and between southwest and west, while the cross streets, which have been called after states, run $22^{1/2}$ degrees west of north, and east of south. Running almost parallel with the sea, are Pacific, Atlantic (the principal street), Arctic, Baltic, Mediterranean and Adriatic avenues. The other streets, twenty-nine in number, are named after the states, in geographical order, beginning at Maine.

The City grows every year, and commerce is to a certain extent making its inroads upon the resident sleepers. A very large business is done in shipping the salt hay of the meadows to New York city, where it is employed for purposes of paper making and horse feed.

Twelve miles from Atlantic City, is the celebrated Mullier river, between which and New York, a propeller makes regular trips, carrying glass, wool and other articles of New Jersey manufacture. New railroad facilities are at present on the tapis. A charter has been obtained for the building of a railroad between Absecon Inlet and Great Egg Harbor Inlet. This work, when finished, will run through the centre of the Island, and will confer additional benefits upon Atlantic City. A turnpike, too, is now building between Atlantic City and Pleasantville, by which, in a short time, there will be a complete road between Philadelphia and the beach.

The principal amusement of Atlantic City, is of course, bathing. This will not be much information for the reader, but our object being to make a guide as well as a history, it must not be objected to that we have introduced matters of such common concern.

The beach is lined during the season with temporary bathing structures, but such is the force and inland reach of the tide-swell during the winter, that it becomes imperative to remove them beyond high water mark; and a few weeks before the summer season opens, the beach presents an animated scene of busy laborers, who are engaged in digging out from the accumulated sand drifts, the debris and ruins of scattered bath-houses. The winter of 1866-67 was unusually severe, and the swell of the tide extended nearly to Atlantic avenue, a distance of four hundred yards from the beach. All along the beach of the Inlet there is splendid fishing, at which amusement, many gentlemen find more pleasure than in playing with the breakers. At low water, there is a splendid drive for ten miles along the surf, and carriages are always easily obtained at reasonable rates.

A good view can always be obtained from the lighthouse, but visitors desirous of observing a fine expanse of seacoast, should visit Dr. Pitney, at Absecon. From the cupola of the Doctor's residence, there is visible on a clear day, upwards of thirty-five miles of coast.

The two beaches, *i.e.* Absecon and Brigantine, are about equal in extent, each being about ten miles in length. On Brigantine beach, about four miles from Atlantic City, there occurred five years ago, a fearful tragedy. This is the only cold-blooded murder that has marred the simple quietude of the place. How many may be committed in the future it is impossible to tell, but let us hope that this Turner tragedy may be the first and last.

Turner was an oysterman. One Gandy followed the same business. The former attended to his occupation, and was successful. He made the rocks with a degree of celerity that caused the jealous soul of Gandy, who worked hard but raised no "stamps," to swell, until it reached the dimensions of the spiritual portion of the celebrated Mr. Gloster's construction. The green-eyed monster now transmogrified the quiet going Gandy into a combination of Dr. Webster, Dick the three, and Lucretia Borgia's henchman. With his soul thus fortified, he was prepared for a final clash to retrieve his fortune, or to use a new quotation "perish in the attempt."

Dick aforesaid, was however, a respectable life-taker, compared with the miserable hero of this bloody, brigandish business on Brigantine Beach. Richard was a polite and elegant murderer. He could send men to take pleasant and comfortable lodgings in the tower, that William the Norman originated in the shape of a fortress. When Dick's victims were enjoying the luxuries and pleasures of secluded retirement in the aforesaid place, Richard used to employ common *cases* to do the finishing part of murderous manufacture. Even the tool Tyrrel, was not such a low individual as Mr. Gandy. Then again, Dr. Webster did the business in a scientific and professional manner, by the use of, in the first place, the Lord knows what, and in the second place, a laboratory furnace. This was simply the reduction of man to his natural elements, and a striking scientific proof of the indestructibility, if not of matter, certainly of teeth. Even the janitor, to whom Doctor W. gave a turkey, in commemoration of his exploit, was a gentleman compared to Mr. Gandy. Lucretia Borgia was a fine woman in many respects, and though her poisoner was a scamp, she said Mr. Gandy was a good deal *scamper*.

Townsend, the brave and heroic highway robber, who, ten years ago, scared the simple-minded Scotchmen of Upper Canada from Toronto to Sandwich, was respected in his generation, for he only embarked in the killing business, when self defence necessitated his "observation of the case in those lamps." All these combined, would not make such a mean miscreant as Brigantine Gandy. But we have been hitherto enlarging on the subject without hitting it, and this last is an important matter, for if you don't hit your subject, you are no account to the reader. The fault now-a-days is, that so few hit their subject where they ought to. Members of Congress are requested to take notice of this last remark, and govern their peculiarly *spoiled* selves accordingly. Here we are at last arrived at the

BRIGANTINE MURDER.

Turner had succeeded so well, that he had managed to build himself a comfortable house upon a spot, at that part of the lower end of Brigantine Beach that was most favorable for carrying on the business of an oysterman. By dint of energy and perseverance, he had managed to accumulate a small amount of money, which he hid underneath the earth, below a board in the floor of his neat but small habitation. Gandy, who had been unsuccessful in the business of an oysterman, had been taken into the confidence of Turner. Now, Gandy was an older man than Turner, and could not bear that the more energetic, but younger individual should exceed him in the possession of oysterial wealth. The result of these agitations produced a determination in the breast of Gandy to transcend all laws, in the hope of winning revenge. Accordingly, one dark and stormy night, while the wind whistled and the thunder rolled—while the lightning flashed, and all the artillery of the "unending heavens" burst forth in wild, malignant fury, this arch-fiend fired the peaceful home of the Turner family, and by the foul deed murdered two individuals he intended to save. Exasperated beyond measure by being cheated of his prey, he fired his remaining shot at the daughter of Turner, and wounded her fearfully in the arm. The wretch next performed the most sensible part of the tragedy that was possible, and after having put off to sea in a skiff, he wisely chose the *nobile letum Catonis*, and by the wholesome application of a little powder and ball, he succeeded in depositing his animal brains upon the skiff's bottom. His last words were "Revenge is sweet." He did not say that

"Revenge was a delicacy of life," for those words were not in his vocabulary. He was, however, cheated of much of his revenge, for the daughter of Turner, whom he left for dead, still lives, a "prosperous lady." This is the only murder that has occurred upon this beach since its original settlement by the Caucasian race.

CHAPTER IX.

GROWTH OF COUNTRY ON RAILROAD LINE.

As has been already stated, the country through which the line of railroad was surveyed, was for the greater part an almost unbroken wilderness. That enterprise, however, which is always consequent upon the consummation of such a work, was soon infused into the sleeping population. After leaving Camden, in one of the commodious six new passenger cars that have been built this season, the first stopping place of the train, is the antiquated but interesting town of Haddonfield, which has improved in a great degree, though not in the same ratio as the other villages upon the railroad line.

The principal reason for this, is, that Haddonfield, by reason of both its shady situation and picturesque simplicity, has always presented a pleasing place for the erection of private villas. Thriving city men, who desired that their families should be brought up sufficiently far from the city to enjoy the delights of life among rural demesnes, and sufficiently near, to place comparative luxuries within easy reach, were not slow to turn the advantages of such a place to good account. Thus,

Haddonfield, with its surrounding farms, holding a population of nearly two thousand souls, may be set down as a delightful adjunct to the suburbs of Philadelphia. The result of Haddonfield's becoming a place of residence, rather than a spot wherein to transact business, was, that no manufactories, such as exist in other Jersey towns, are found there. Agriculture, however, and stock-raising, have been well attended to all along the Haddonfield tract. Mr. Charles H. Shinn has long lived a lusty *rus in urbe* life, and with truly Roman pride, such as was possessed by the brave husbandman Dictators of old, feels happier in the simple pleasures of superintending his unparalleled Alderneys, than he does in his counting house in Philadelphia. His son, Captain Shinn, who has gained no little distinction on many a well fought battlefield during the recent conflict, is one of the most respected of Philadelphia's merchants, and ranks among the honored local celebrities of Haddonfield.

Messrs. Collins, Kay, Walton, Willetts, Joseph Withers and Hopkins, are among the principal villa owners. Among the other prominent citizens, are Judge Clements, a man with a whole soul (which is a rare thing in the present era of the world), Colonel Peyton and Captain Sower. The two last are "war-worn veterans." We had almost forgotten the genial Dr. Burnell and the witty Edwin P. Graham. When the last named gentleman puffs his cigar and "quaffs his exhilarations," in the evening, after the clouds of night dim the dome that rests upon the forest trees, then will the starry stillness be broken by the sparkling flashes of Edwin's jocularity.

*　　　*　　　*　　　*　　　*　　　*

There is a sad story in the annals of Haddonfield—
we did not hear it from a native of that place—indeed we
much doubt whether any present resident of Haddonfield
could give the correct version of the tragic tale. We heard
it from an oysterman, who probably told it to feed his
own vanity, and kept repeating it to feed the vanity of his
brother oysterists, and minister to their pleasure.

Many years ago there lived upon Absecon beach, an
oysterman named Thomas Durch. He accumulated a small
fortune, the product of close attention to his businesss,
and gave his only son, whom he called for Thomas
Jefferson, an excellent primary education. The boy early
showed an aptitude for business, and was steadily making
his way in life, when he undertook to make a journey to
New York. On his tour, as luck would have it, he was
obliged to remain at the hotel in Haddonfield, for a period
of about a fortnight. There chanced to be stopping at the
same hotel a middle-aged lady with her daughter. Thomas
Jefferson Durch made considerable advancement towards
winning the young lady's affection, during his short stay.
An attachment sprang up between the young people.
They corresponded. Her father and mother approved the
union, till such time as her "governor's" name came to
be mentioned as a probable candidate for Congress in
Ohio. This turned the old fellow's head so completely,
that he could no longer hear of the daughter of a
probable Congresser being married to the son of a low
oysterman. The would-be parliamentarian consequently intercepted the love letters between the parties, and

ordered all further notions of matrimony to be dispelled from his daughter's mind. In this plight, Miss Augusta Haberdasher left her father's house one night. After a long and wearisome journey, during which she required all her ingenuity to save herself from becoming a victim to the "oft repeated vigilance" of the *posse comitatus*, she at last arrived at the same hotel in Haddonfield, where she first met her Thomas Jefferson, *etc., etc.* She expected to find some letters for her, as she had directed Thomas, that in the event of any thing happening to interfere with their communications, he should write her at this hotel, where she would be sure to come in due time. She accordingly enquired for the desired missives, and was handed a batch of william-duxes. She read them through with the avidity usual, under such circumstances, and was making up her mind to visit her intended, when the hoarse voice of the landlord was heard to exclaim: "Miss Gussy, another letter—somebody dead, I reckon—black edge!" She broke the seal with trembling hands, and read:

Theas is to infurm yer, that mi sun Tomus shot hisself last nite becoz he hadint got no word from yer for a long time. Theas lines were ritt by a saler boy.

his

TOMUS x DURCH.

Mark.

NOTIS—The Blak Eghe Cover wuz in Tomus' box.

Augusta did not swoon, neither did she cry. She however, made a pilgrimage to the beach and attempted to drown herself, but finding drowning more unpleasant than she anticipated, she called to a wrecker to "save her or she'd perish," which he magnanimously did. She lived to marry a mutton-pie man, who afterwards became a United States Senator, and let us hope she lived and died happily in spite of the sad memories that haunted her when her mind wandered to the sacred scenes that clustered around Haddonfield—those scenes that must have changed the glory of her heart's setting sun into a twilight of sad feelings, in the latter years of her life.— This story in the above unconnected and rambling form, is precisely as the above-mentioned person related it to the writer. With these few remarks, we bid *adieu* to Haddonfield.   *   *   *   *

Sixteen and a-half miles from Camden, is the village of Long-a-Coming, which fourteen years ago contained three houses and a barn. The present population is upwards of four hundred.

Twenty-three miles from Camden, we strike Waterford, a thriving town, sustained by a glass manufactory, and possessing a population of four hundred and fifty. Before the building of the railway, there were not more than eighty people in the settlement.

Twenty-seven miles from Camden, stands the enterprising settlement of Winslow, which is also supported by factories. The population, which now amounts to seven hundred and fifty, was not more than two hundred souls in 1856.

Absecon village, where Dr. Pitney, the prominent pioneer resides, originally had but sixty inhabitants. The population in 1867 was upwards of one hundred and seventy-five.

Along this line was the settlement of Jackson, about a mile and a-half from the railroad. The village's transportation facilities are now supplied by Jackson station, twenty miles from Camden. Glass manufacture has been for some time successfully carried on in this locality. The inhabitants of Jackson settlement, originally numbered three hundred and sixty-five. Near Jackson, were the *colonies* Gibbsborough, Tansboro, Weymouth, Ironworks and Mays Landing. The aggregate number of people who occupied these crude villages was about one thousand. Besides these settlements, there was a narrow strip of land on both sides of the country roads running nearly parallel with, and from a quarter of a mile, to two miles distant from, the railroad. Along this strip, to the distance of about twenty-seven miles from Camden, there were for a long time no improvements in the then temporary settlements of wood-choppers. This portion of the country was, fifteen years ago, little better than a home for deer, foxes, bears, pheasants and those cunning, amiable, pretty not to say delightful little insects, known under the appellation of mosquitoes. The cultivation of the soil was utterly neglected, and attention was only given to working off the wood with which that region eminently abounded. This wood business was profitable, inasmuch as a speedy market was always found in New York city for anything in the shape of cord-wood.

This wretched state of things no longer exists. The forests have been to a great extent cleared away, and the stumping machines have finished the business. New settlements are continually forming, and the old ones are rapidly increasing in wealth and population. New districts are being brought under efficient cultivation, and the original farmers are adding to, and improving their agricultural facilities.

The Hammonton tract, upon which, at the opening of the road, there were but some thirty residents, now comfortably, and in some instances affluently supports twenty-five hundred permanent inhabitants. These people are the occupants of farms, of from twenty to one hundred acres, which are rapidly being brought to a high state of husbandry, and upon which, extensive and productive orchards and vineyards are always planted. The houses erected by the settlers are neat and comfortable. In their internal arrangements, as well as in their dealing, the people evince the neatness, exactness and "cent-savingness" of the sturdy, stiff New England people, who predominate in this part of New Jersey. Hence, from having retained their original characteristics, and from their present place of residence, Philadelphians have concocted the phrase, "Jersey Yankee," to indicate one that is "keener on a trade" than even the present denizens of the land of pure cold water and wooden nutmegs.

This whole section of country will, in five years, do honor to the name of Jersey, and will abundantly prove itself worthy of being called for a channel island. It will be a complete garden spot, and in addition, it will become as valuable an agricultural section as any of the same extent in the country. Its value will be materially enhanced by the wide parallel roads, that have been laid out at regular intervals.

This projected regularity pervades a section of country, which extends twenty miles in length, along the line of the Camden and Atlantic Railroad. In breadth, these demesnes of improvement reach Little Egg Harbor river on the north side, a distance of more than six miles, and on the southwest, in some points to Great Egg Harbor river.

Egg Harbor City's present condition, as well as that of the Hammonton tract upon which the town is built, exhibits the great results that are always to be looked for, from the judicious employment of capital, and its energetic concentration. When the first train ran over the railway, on the 1st of July, 1854, there were upon this entire section but five wretchedly supported families. The tract now feeds a thriving population of eighteen hundred.

The improvements, however, are not confined to this portion of the country. The lands most accessible from the stations of Waterford, Winslow, Da Costa and Weymouth, are now offered for sale, and are being rapidly bought up. Already cultivation has been commenced upon some of them, and in a few instances extensive preparations have been made, of such a nature as shall allure the settler.

When we consider that until very recently, the greater part of these lands was not offered for sale at all—that they rested under the reproach of being valueless, and withal "out of the United States"—when, too, we remember the stagnation of business and the financial revulsions that the road has withstood—when we regard all this, such results are of a most extraordinary as well as of a most encouraging character. Since this region of country has been extensively advertised, and attention has been generally directed to it; and since its value has been practically demonstrated, we confidently expect that its rare advantages will not "go a-begging" in the future. In fact, the railway people anticipate the settlement of portions of this land by at least an addition of twelve hundred inhabitants during the ensuing year. Great as are these improvements, they convey a very inadequate conception of what has been accomplished upon the line of railroad. The production of all lands, that run close upon the railroad, has, within five years, increased in value by fifty per cent. The spirit which has operated to produce these more prominent results, is also evinced in the renovation and enrichment of the old farms, which are within reach of the influence exerted immediately upon the railroad line.

Atlantic City itself, requires little mention in this connection. Its rapid improvements, and the immense number of visitors who throng there during the summer months, is the strongest possible evidence of its inherent adaptation for the purposes for which it was founded. Its land has improved in value, with a rapidity that was never known anywhere before. The property for which Dr. Pitney, only sixteen years ago, paid seventeen *dollars* an *acre*, cannot be purchased to-day for less than that sum per *foot*.

CHAPTER X.

Hot Weather Theatricals.

Don't start gentle reader, at the peculiar heading of this chapter! Atlantic City has its summer theatricals, for indeed any other kind would be of no use. The usual performances that are produced upon the actual boards in other localities during the dramatic season, would not be graced (graced is the word—*Sampson Brass*) by any sort of appropriative audiences, were they (the performances, not the audiences) conducted within gas-lit halls, under the stage management of hoary headed Winter. The audiences would not distinguish Sir Charles Coldsteam from his *laquais*; they would return to their respective homes, in considerable doubt as to whether Terry the Swell was Sir Wilton Downe, or *vice versa*. We can easily imagine a crowd of Atlanticese wending its way from a dramatic exhibition, with a confusion of mind very much resembling the condition of heaven, hell, earth and chaos, as described by one of the inspired people who flourished in the poetic past. Winter would be a bad manager for the place. He would always be "busted up" at the end of the season, and after trying a second time, he would unfortunately discover that he had been fighting with the dire decrees of an Irishman's providence.

The Atlantic theatricals are always placed upon "imaginary boards" and for the most part, are the comic, sentimental and gushing phases of positive existence. The most interesting and entertaining of them are such as take place

IN THE WATER.

The star bather is performing—she swims like a chick—at the hop scenes she cuts a better *figure*—*in aqua*, she belongs to the *ordo pancakius*—she is a low comedian and all laugh at her—she is middle-aged. What means the black ribbon tied beneath her chin? why is not her rich hair "unfurled to the breeze?" Poor creature! she has none to furl or unfurl; visitors, however, are kept in ignorance of this fact; the *ordo pancakius* she don't mind, for she goes to Atlantic to bathe. Noble exhibition of heroic womanism!

Noise, and her twin sister, Pleasure, are in the ascendant—there is noise with the waves, noise in the water, noise with the surge, noise with the breakers, noise with the surf, noise with the bathers, noise on the shore. The crowds scamper in the waves and yell continually, but as each, his share of noise contributes, none are annoyed. Ancient Mr. Sol is attired in his accustomed splendour, and the fact must be admitted that *in propria persona*, he sheds more light upon the aquarial theatricals than was ever known to be thrown upon the unimaginary boards by the usual appliances. The "star" bather is in *medias res* of an excellent swim. The youngsters jocosely splash each other. The sounds are all of revelry by day—all is lovely as a water lilly.

When "Hush! Hark! do you not see a shark?"[*] "No!" 'Twas but a water speck or a simple sail ploughing the glassy deep. On with the bath, let noise be unannoyed. No end of watery joy till dinner bells do ring, to tell us there awaits our hungry selves, roast beef and wines, to chase the nasty indigestion from our craving stomachs. On with the fun! But hold, again! that speck upon the water grows, and moves while growing towards the bathers. It seems as though Destruction had marked some for his own.

The fear increases. The danger every moment becomes more and more apparent. The juveniles cling to their natural protectors. The nurses, that line the shore along, forget their little charges in the tumultuous throng, and many a child is *dropped* while wild and high, the breakers roll, and lustily the bathers roar.

*   *   *   *   *   *   *

The last minute beheld them full of aquarial glee— the last moment in conglomerate ease, and free—now separate from danger, they gaze in charming *dishabile*, gaze from the shore in wonder real, and scan the contour of the confounded shark. Curiosity ripens—the shark approaches. The people never before wondered more. Mr. Sol, for a short moment, dims his glory behind a vapory cloud, ends the suspense and discloses to the deluded optics of the consternists, the unpleasant fact that the shark has disappeared, and that the object which "created so much fuss," was but a speck made large by the reflection of the *daylight's major*.

* The shark that "appeared" in the summer of 1859, and created so much excitement among the bathers was only a myth.

THE HOP SCENES.

The hop (that is the Latin, Greek or Hebrew word for a ball) is the greatest performance of the season. Each hotel must organize its *corps de hoppet*, or else it cannot be considered a first-class establishment.

THE DOG, GUN AND LINE.

Since the interposition of Attic Providence saved Rome (and some time before), the quacking species has been of peculiar interest to sportsmen. These individuals make seasonable progresses *Be d'akeon para thina*, as John Cypress might have said. Their dog goes with them *Be d'akeon*, &c. They find a "thatchy spot," and recline *sub gramine* till grey morn bids them commence operations. The inlet affords amusement to flytailers, who were described by Dr. Johnson as being at one end of a piece of machinery, while at the other was a hook.

We cannot conclude this book without recording the hope that, if one of our admiring readers should ever be found in the same predicament as we once beheld a young damsel in the water, and should conclude to repeat that lady's prayer, a speedy answer may be vouchsafed her.

She had, previously to her miserable situation, been reading "Childe Harold" and "The Fire Worshippers." She was sweet sixteen, and upon this occasion stood up to her neck in the ocean; while she was in this position, she beheld upon the shore, a young, fine looking, favorite stage manager from Versailles. It was her affinity she thought, for she had yearned for such a one for a long time. Casting her eyes out toward the broad expanse of sea beyond the bar, and at the same time assuming a poetic expression, she apostrophised the combined concussion thuswise:

> "Ye elements, in whose ennobling stir
> I feel myself exalted—can ye not
> Accord me such a being?"

(THE CURTAIN FALLS.)

Report says not what answer the prayer received, but those who may be desirous of further information, are respectfully referred to Madame Keckley, unless they are willing to bide their time, until the dark lady's new handbook of private gossip be put upon the market in due form.

FOLLOW THE MONEY
THE RHETORIC OF PROMOTION
IN CARNESWORTHE'S *ATLANTIC CITY*

————

The author behind the pseudonym is Alexander Barrington Irvine, and this is apparently his only book-length work. He arrived in Philadelphia in the late 1860s and for a few years served as editor of *The Philadelphia and Southern Trade Journal*, a pro free-enterprise publication. Both the *Journal* and *Atlantic City* were published by Wm. C. Harris & Co.

This book fits easily within the genre of railroad promotional literature, popular in the middle of the nineteenth century. It is less a history as its full title advertises and more a clever marketing tool. Wm. C. Harris & Co. would have benefited if sales were robust, and the Camden and Atlantic Railroad, so wholeheartedly championed by Irvine, also stood to profit, as did the companion entity, the Camden and Atlantic Land Company.

Bad timing may have impacted its reception. Railroad historian James A. Ward argues that by the late 1860s public sentiment had begun to turn against railroad promotions which had come to hold negative associations. In order to stir public passion and rally financial support for projects, authors had used "a multitude of rhetorical approaches calculated to graft railways to broad, commonly held political and cultural assumptions" (Ward 70). Their language was "fraught with symbolism," bonding readers to the new industry and suggesting an optimistic future. At the same time, railroad companies also used their considerable influence to dampen prospective competition.

Irvine, while paid for his boosterism, *was* a capable writer. His narrative voice conveys an ironic, yet optimistic tone, balancing romantic stories, factual detail, and blunt marketing. He makes use of various literary styles, and while often calculating, is always pleasing.

Pro-business sympathies color the unflattering portrayal of South Jersey natives as primitives hopelessly disadvantaged until the fortunate arrival of the railroad, lighthouse, and beach resort. "Before the railroad existed, the people of Absecon village employed themselves in the primitive occupation of carting oysters sixty miles to Camden, through the sands of Jersey" (41). Observations throughout the text are shaped for their promotional value.

Still, it is a mistake to read *Atlantic City* as a single-minded advertisement for nineteenth-century capitalism. Irvine's arch storytelling, presented through the persona of Carnesworthe, is entertaining and delivers a high-spirited, if not wholly accurate, origin tale for the Jersey Shore.

Stefanie Schulte

Ward, James A. "Promotional Wizardry: Rhetoric and Railroad Origins, 1820-1860." *Journal of the Early Republic* 11.1 (Spring 1991): 69-88.

Colophon

This edition of Carnesworthe's *Atlantic City*, reset from the orginal, was edited by Stephanie Allen, Ryan Ballard, Stefanie Schulte, Jessica Walkowich, and Daniel Weir. Additional editing was provided by Victoria Conover (of the Absecon Conovers). Publication was supervised by Tom Kinsella. Thanks to Joseph Felcone and Paul W. Schopp for their encouragement and help. David Munn suggested this project and gave us access to his first edition: for that we give him special thanks.

The text is set in 12 point Garamond, table of contents in 9 point Corbel, and chapter headings in 20 point Century. Pagination does not follow the original edition. Cover design by Sarah Messina.

South Jersey Culture & History Center